The Definitive Guide to Sales Cadence

HOW TO DOUBLE YOUR CONTACT RATES IN LESS THAN 30 DAYS

GABE LARSEN
VP OF GROWTH

INSIDE
SALES
.COM

TABLE OF CONTENTS

---

05 INTRODUCTION

07 THE FIVE ELEMENTS OF A SALES CADENCE

15 CALLS

19 VOICEMAIL

23 EMAIL

31 SOCIAL MEDIA

37 DIRECT MAIL

39 TEXTING

41 EXAMPLE CADENCES

49 SCORE YOUR CADENCE

51 TRY PLAYBOOKS

Introduction

Every sales representative executes a 'cadence' when they reach out via email, phone, or social media to initiate a conversation with a potential prospect. The art of a cadence is determined based on a myriad of factors, fueled primarily by sales reps' intuition regarding the company and contact being pursued. However, there are a lot of questions that aren't always clear when initiating a conversation and creating a successful cadence.

- How many times should I attempt contact?
- How long should I wait between attempts?
- What methods are most likely to result in a conversation?
- What messaging will resonate with my potential buyer?
- When should I give up?

These are only a few of the many questions sales reps consider when creating their optimal cadence.

Because these cadences are built purely on intuition, the answers to the above questions introduce a variety of answers – many of which limit a sales rep's ability to effectively turn prospects into potential buyers.

- Place one call too many, and you tick off your lead or contact.
- Give up too soon on someone, and you will turn up short on quota.
- Use the wrong the communication method and you'll fail to get a response

So, what is the right cadence and how should companies begin building them?

I run our InsideSales Labs team, the research and best practice arm of InsideSales.com and we've spent the last 12 months cracking the code on cadence. We've come up with a more clear definition and uncovered five critical components for a successful cadence.

Now, just to make sure you don't think we are making this up, let me get you in on a little secret about the data we analyzed to come up with the findings we'll be highlighting in this book.

THE DEFINITION OF A SALES CADENCE

A sales cadence is vital to your sales strategy. It's the path a sales rep follows to success, and when it's implemented correctly, a sales cadence can nearly double your contact rates. Our definition of a sales cadence is a sequence of activities that increases contact and qualification rates.

When cadences are performed correctly, they not only increase a rep's ability to engage with a prospect, but they also educate buyers further down the sales pipeline.

Inbound Cadences

An inbound cadence is when a rep reaches out to someone who knows your company with a certain sequence of sales activities. In our research, we've studied over 14,000+ cadences, made up of 144,000+ total activities, across nearly 9,000 companies. (Please note the inbound leads we studied were considered high scoring leads as they came from web forms such as contact us, free trial, and demo request. Not all inbound leads are created equal so the findings in this paper will focus on what reps do and should do to optimize their interaction with high priority inbound leads).

Outbound Cadences

An outbound cadence is when a rep reaches out to someone who doesn't know your company via email, phone or other methods of communication. In our research we've studied more than 1.5 million activities across 479,140 outbound cadences.

The Five Elements of a Sales Cadence[*]

Most sales leaders measure their sales teams' productivity by the number of contact attempts per lead. While volume is an important part to a sales rep's success, when it comes to effective cadences, the number of attempts is only one piece of the puzzle. Here are the five key elements of a successful sales cadence:

ATTEMPTS   The total number of touch points made

MEDIA   The type of communication methods used

DURATION   The time between the first and last attempt

SPACING   The time gap between contact attempts

CONTENT   The messaging used

Let's dive into each of these briefly to understand them in more detail.

THE STRUCTURE OF A SALES CADENCE

When deciding the structure of a cadence you need to review five elements:

Attempts

This is the total number of touches on a lead or contact. We performed a survey and asked over 1000 companies how many touches they executed on a lead or contact and the the total number was 15.4.

That 15.4 breaks down to 4.7 calls, 4.6 emails, 2.9 voicemails, 1.8 social touches, 0.8 mailers, 0.7 text messages. But that's what they 'said' they did. What did they really do, and how many attempts should someone actually make?

When we examined what reps actually did we found that, analyzing InsideSales.com's big data[1], the typical inbound cadence has 4.05 attempts and the typical outbound cadence has 3 attempts. There is clearly a disconnect between what people say they do versus what they actually do.

What should be the total amount of touches? In the old days, the number you would hear was 8-10, but for the most part that was just made up by people who felt like they knew what was best. What data tells us is that for inbound cadences you can do up to ten total attempts with the sweet spot at six attempts and for an outbound cadence you should do up to six total attempts with the sweet spot being at three attempts. Going past these numbers is not necessary bad, it's is just less effective.

It's important to note the data we studied only included phone, voicemail, and email. With that said, it is our belief that including other mediums such as social, mailers, and text messages is extremely helpful. As a recommendation, we would suggest the following which includes all communication methods:

1) CADENCE AUDIT 2017
https://www.insidesales.com/research-paper/
sales-cadences-thousands-companies

Inbound:

Phone, VM, Email = up to 10 touches

Phone, VM, Email, Social, Direct Mail, Text = up to 10 touches

Outbound:

Phone, VM, Email = up to 7 touches

Phone, VM, Email, Social, Direct Mail, Text = up to 8 touches

Media

This is the media pattern used. You can get very creative with media. You can only use phone calls or only send emails or you can use a combination of the two as well as other forms of communication.

The key with media is to remember there are six types of communication methods you can use for prospecting:

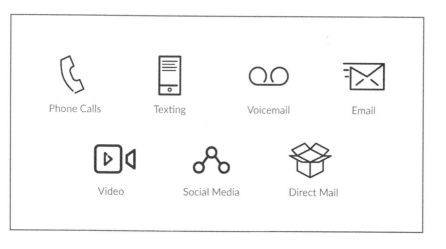

Phone Calls	Texting	Voicemail	Email
Video	Social Media	Direct Mail	

Voicemail and video have been debated as communication methods as they both use other mediums to communicate their message. Although that may be true, both of them play a big role in how reps communicate to prospects so we opted to put both them in.

When we examined inbound cadences, we found the most used media was a single email with 31.6% of all cadences following this approach. It's boring, I get it but this is where most sales reps stop. The five most popular inbound cadences were:

Email	✉
Call - Voicemail	☏ – ☎
Email - Email	✉ – ✉
Call - Voicemail - Email	☏ – ☎ – ✉
Email - Email - Email	✉ – ✉ – ✉

When we looked at most optimal cadences, for inbound the most successful cadence was Call - Voicemail - Email repeated between 6-10 touches. Unfortunately this combination was only used 4.7% of the time. The idea of using multiple communication methods to see success is not new.

Our research has shown time and again that using multiple communication methods is always more effective than using just one:

- one communication method: 9.5% success rate
- two communication methods: 22.5% success rate
- three communication methods: 25.1% success rate

That's a big difference in your ability to have a conversation when using a single communication method versus three communication methods (165.9% higher).

When we examined outbound sales cadences, it was completely different than inbound when it came to media. The most utilized outbound sales cadence was a single dial, with 26.5% of all cadences following this pattern.

But, just because it was heavily used, it doesn't mean it was optimal.

Here are the top five most optimal outbound sales cadences:

Call - Call - Call - Call - Email - Call	☏ - ☏ - ☏ - ☏ - ✉ - ☏
Email - Call - Call - Call - Call - Call	✉ - ☏ - ☏ - ☏ - ☏ - ☏
Call - Call - Call - Email - Call - Call	☏ - ☏ - ☏ - ✉ - ☏ - ☏
Call - Call - Email - Call - Call - Call	☏ - ☏ - ✉ - ☏ - ☏ - ☏
Call - Email - Call - Call - Call - Call	☏ - ✉ - ☏ - ☏ - ☏ - ☏

When it comes to using different communication methods, you should figure out what works best for you and your audience, but here are a few principles you should consider:

- Phone is 2x more popular than email (65.6% of all activities for phone versus 31.8% all activities)

- The more communication methods, typically the better

- Reps who follow up on inbound leads should focus more on aggressive methods such as the phone. This is especially true if this is a transactional sale where deals are smaller and sales cycles are faster.

- Reps who go outbound to target contacts and accounts should start with more passive communication such as email or social, followed by more aggressive communication like the phone. This is especially true if this is a relational sale where deals are larger and sales cycles are slower.

You'll note that the above examples only include phone, voicemail, and email due to lack of data for other forms of communication. Using social, video, direct mailers, and text messages can be very effective in both inbound and outbound cadences.

Transactional vs. Relational Sales

Transactional

In this sales model, the sales rep gets in touch with a lead and simply tries to close a sale without trying to build a relationship with the prospect. Every deal has a small number of decision makers (1-3), deals have a short sales cycle of < 90 days, and deal sizes are under $32,000.

Relational

Relational sales are better suited for sales in large companies with over 100 employees, and where deal sizes are over $32,000. The sales rep needs to build relationships inside the company, which means that the sales cycles are a bit longer (>90 days), and you need to build rapport with more decision makers (+4) than in a transactional sales cycle.

Duration

Duration is the time between the first and last attempt.

1000+ companies reported the average duration was 29.3 days for a sales cadence. Again, when we analyzed the InsideSales.com data set for inbound leads, we found the actual duration was at 4.89 days, but when looking at outbound cadences the duration was 20.8 days which was much closer to the perceived average.

When analyzing what cadences performed the best for inbound and outbound leads or contacts, the durations were not far apart.

For inbound leads, reps should have cadences that last up to ten days, while outbound target accounts should last up to twelve days. Like attempts, it is not necessarily bad to go past these date ranges, it is just less effective.

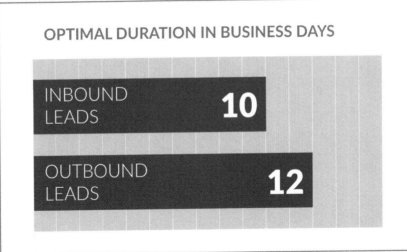

OPTIMAL DURATION IN BUSINESS DAYS

INBOUND LEADS **10**

OUTBOUND LEADS **12**

CADENCE AUDIT 2017
https://www.insidesales.com/research-paper/
sales-cadences-thousands-companies

Spacing

Spacing is the time between activities. Spacing is the most overlooked element of a cadence.

In our study, companies reported the average spacing for cadence activities was 1.9 days. Most sales reps believe cadence spacing should fall between one and four days but some feel it should extend to a week or two. When we studied the data, for inbound leads the typical spacing was 4.23 days, which is quite a bit higher than people believed they were doing. Reps often feel they are bugging prospects, so we were not surprised to see the disconnected in what people do versus what they say they do. Interestingly, the time gap after the first contact attempt was the shortest (16 hours, 45 minutes) and each gap got longer until reps finally settled into a weekly spacing pattern.

To stay in optimal spacing ranges on inbound leads, reps should have spacing up to two days.

Outbound cadences acted similar to inbound cadences when it came to spacing. For outbound cadences, the average spacing was 4.5 days and like the inbound cadences, the optimal spacing was up to 2 days.

OPTIMAL SPACING IN BUSINESS DAYS

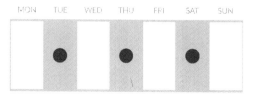

| MON | TUE | WED | THU | FRI | SAT | SUN |

Content

Content is the messaging used within a cadence.

Don't confuse content with what you say when you actually make contact with an individual. Content in this instance is the messaging used in emails, texts, voicemails, videos, and direct mailers to initiate contact or educate your buyer. Content can be the x-factor in a cadence as a rep can send one really good email and the rest of the cadence may not be necessary.

When it comes to optimal content structures and strategies, we will review those in details in the below sections, but let me discuss some data points regarding content that might be of interest.

The typical prospecting email is 362 words and nearly half of voicemails were over 30 seconds. When analyzing best practices across both inbound and outbound, the optimal length of an email varied, but emails with less than 300 words did perform better than emails with over 300 words. There is a debate among many sales reps about the optimal length of an email. Some argue for extremely short emails, while others argue for long-form emails. At this point, we do not have the best answer for this using data.

When it came to voice messages, the data showed that voicemails under 30 seconds perform better than those that were over 30 seconds long.

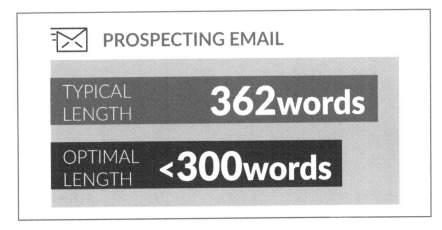

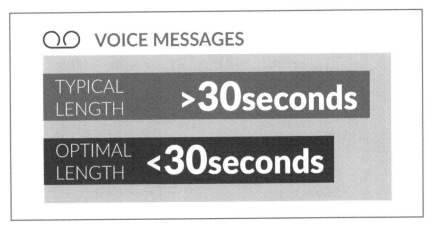

Calls

With the sequence in place, we're ready to focus on step five - plays. Let's first look at phone call plays as part of your cadence. The average lead is only called 1.5 times. That's not going to cut it, but what is? We did a study[2] in conjunction with the Harvard Business Review that examined over 100,000 phone calls. The purpose of the study was to determine what are best practices around calling cadences.

The study answered five key questions:

 What is the best day to call?

 What is the optimal time to call?

 How fast should you respond to inbound leads

 Is an out-of-state area code better or worse than a local area code?

 What is the optimal number of phone calls?

Let's review the answers.

2) BEST PRACTICES FOR LEAD RESPONSE MANAGEMENT
https://www.insidesales.com/insider/lead-management/
lead-response-management-infographic/

PHONE BEST PRACTICES

What is the Best Day to Call?

Believe it or not, it's Wednesday and Thursday. There is a 49.7% difference in contact rates between Thursday and the worst day, Tuesday. Interestingly, Wednesdays and Thursdays are also the best days to call to qualify leads. Wednesday was the top day and it was 24.9% better than the worst day, which was Friday. Why is this? When I spoke to busy decision makers they said Monday and Tuesday are spent digging themselves out of the weekend traffic and Friday they try to get out of work early.

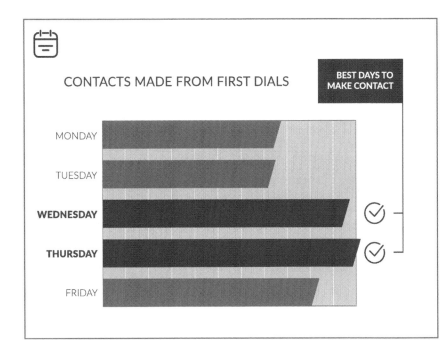

CONTACTS MADE FROM FIRST DIALS

BEST DAYS TO MAKE CONTACT

MONDAY
TUESDAY
WEDNESDAY
THURSDAY
FRIDAY

What is the Optimal Time to Call?

4 to 6pm is the best time to call to make contact with a lead. It is 114% better than calling at 11 to 12pm, right before lunch. 8-9am and 4-5pm are the best times to call to qualify a lead. 8-9am is 164% better than calling at 1-2pm, right after lunch. That's a big difference!

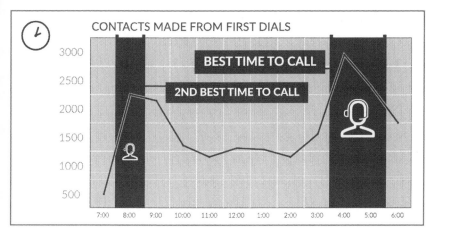

CONTACTS MADE FROM FIRST DIALS

How Fast Should You Respond to Inbound Leads?

The magic number is 5 minutes. You are 100x more likely to contact a lead and 21x more likely to qualify a lead if you contact that lead in under five minutes. This data scares people and truthfully makes some people uncomfortable. "If I contact a lead too fast won't I scare them?" No, actually the most common word when reps respond quickly to a lead is, "Wow". People like to buy from people who hustle and responding in five minutes is hustling.

One note here. Not all leads are created equal. You have to find the balance of speed and priority. If you don't have the capacity to respond to all leads quickly, you should respond to your best leads first.

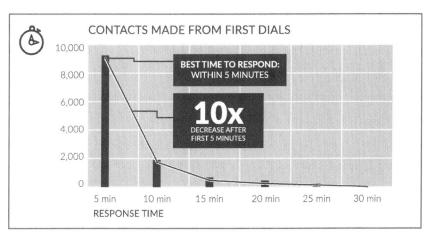

CONTACTS MADE FROM FIRST DIALS

Is an Out of State Area Code Better or Worse than a Local Area Code?

What does this mean? It means when you call a prospect-- how big of an advantage is it to have a local area code number display on the prospect's caller-id? The answer is, it's a pretty big deal. A local phone number has as much as 25% better contact rates than long distance or out of a state area code. That's huge!

What is the Optimal Number of Phone Calls?

Most sales reps get nervous because they don't want to bother people. The average prospect is only called 1.5 times. How many times should you call?

Our data shows that busy decision makers expect to be contacted a lot because they are busy and difficult to get a hold of. As a sales rep, best practice says you want to make six phone calls per lead over the length of your cadence to put your chance of contact up to almost 90%.

Call three is where the magic happens. At call three you increase your chance of contact to almost 80% so truthfully calls four, five, and six do not yield that much more value. For this reason, our foundational cadence recommends you start your cadence with three phone calls.

Voicemail

With phone calls discussed in the last section, next is voice messages. Can you believe that 50-75% of reps don't leave voice messages?

You may not only believe that, but you may be a sales rep who doesn't leave voice messages. Is voicemail dead? It's a fair question, but remember one study on communication methods found that 66.3% of business professionals[3] said they were likely to respond to voicemail.

So the data says it isn't dead, but I do believe some reps have a misconception about what voicemail should and shouldn't do. What is the purpose of a voicemail? Michael Pedone from SalesBuzz says the purpose of the first voicemail is to get a callback and advance the sale.

Reps tell me all the time that when they leave voicemail no one calls them back, so it's not worth leaving them anymore. I tell them to remember that the purpose of a voice mail is not just to get a callback, but also to advance the sale. It's another touch in the process of gaining visibility and educating your audience.

Decision makers get hundreds more emails a day than they do voicemails. A voicemail can be a great way to convey a message and advance the sale.

3) THE EVOLUTION OF BUSINESS COMMUNICATIONS 2017
https://www.insidesales.com/research-paper/evo-
lution-business-communications-2017/

VOICEMAIL BEST PRACTICES

Be Persistent

The magic number of voicemails is three. We analyzed thousands of phone calls both with and without voicemail and we compared the contact rate. After the third voicemail, if you continue leaving messages, you hinder your ability to contact your prospect. Create a cadence and find a way to spread three voicemails over a 10-business day or 20-business day period.

Use Context/Research

Use information gathered in your pre-call research or information gathered from their inbound inquiry.

Ask What You Want

Don't be afraid to ask for what you want and don't beat around the bush.

Repeat Your Information

With an office phone, leave your name and number twice and write your number on a piece of paper so you say it slowly enough that someone else could write it down or an automated system could transcribe it. If you know it's a mobile phone: Don't leave your number at all. They have it.

Personalize the Message

Use the prospect's name two times in your message.

Keep it Short

Keep your voicemail short. 18-30 seconds is the rule. Respect your prospect's time.

Write it Down

Winging it only leads to trouble. Write your voicemails down and practice leaving a professional message.

Stand /Up and Speak

You need energy and enthusiasm and the best way to do that is to stand up when leaving a voicemail.

Provide Just Enough /Information

Only disclose enough information to get a call back. Don't give your whole sales pitch.

Start Different

Don't start with your name and company name. It's a sure sign of a sales person. Rather end with that information.

Reference Other Communication

Reference other forms of communication, such as an email.

Use Automation

Sales reps have a lot to do. Using a mix of pre-recorded voicemails and personalized voicemails can increase effectiveness.

VOICEMAIL STRATEGIES

Okay, with our best practices in place, let's discuss voicemail strategies. Identifying different strategies provides a framework when thinking about your voicemail that can be really helpful in building a cadence.

There are 12 common voicemail strategies, let's discuss just a few of them:

A Referral Voicemail

This is when a colleague, friend, or acquaintance is connected or referred you to this prospect.

Here is an example:

"John,

Ben Johnson and I connected and your name came up as someone who could benefit from the InsideSales.com Sales Acceleration Platform. Let's connect. It's Gabe Larsen with InsideSales.com. {Your Number}. Again, {Your Number}."

Case Study

This is when you use recognized proof stories to help illustrate how you can assist your prospect. Here is a sample voicemail using the case study strategy.

Here is an example:

"Hi John.

We recently helped ABC company double their revenue in 60 days and I wanted to see if we can do the same for you. I can be reached at {Your Number} Again, my name is {Gabe Larsen}, with InsideSales.com at {Your Number}."

Cliffhanger Strategy

This is when you only provide enough information to get a callback. The cliffhanger strategy can be very powerful if you do it right.

Here is an example:

"John,

I saw on your website an issue with your compliance statement. Can we discuss it? {Gabe Larsen here with InsideSales.com. I can be reached at {Your Number}. That number again is {Your Number}."

Remember these are just three of multiple strategies we've identified to be helpful.

Email

With voicemails and phone calls covered, now let's discuss emails. Did you know there are over 205 billion emails sent each day? The typical office worker receives an average of 121 emails each day, and 70% of unanswered emails stop after one attempt.

Email is an important part of your cadence, so we have to get it right. The key with emails is finding the balance between it and other forms of communication. With a lot of automation and the ease of scheduling campaigns, reps are leaning more and more on emails. Resist the temptation to become an email marketer and find a way to use email as just one of the tools in your prospecting tool belt.

FIVE PART EMAIL STRUCTURE

Let's get into the basics of creating an email. We like to keep it simple. There are five parts to structuring a successful email.

Here are the do's and don'ts for each.

> SUBJECT

> INTRO

> BODY

> CALL TO ACTION

> SIGNATURE

Subject

The purpose is to get your email opened, so:

- Do - keep your subject lines short (around 65 characters)
- Do - consider using images, hashtags, glyph and emojis but do so sparingly
- Don't – use salesy words

Most importantly, test your subject lines. This is one of the best benefits of email engagement tools in the sales acceleration space – the ability to test what works and what doesn't is extremely powerful.

Intro

Purpose is to catch attention.

- Do – personalize. Make it about them, not about you
- Do – use the email best practices we discuss in the next section
- Don't – begin with your name and your company name. It's too salesy.

Body

Purpose is to ignite action (click on a link or reply to your email).

- Do - make it brief
- Do – use the email strategies we discuss in the next section
- Don't – be generic
- Don't – make it unbelievable

Call to Action

Purpose is to elicit a next step.

- Do – ask direct questions
- Do – have a clear call to action
- Don't – be soft

Signature

- Do – standout
- Don't – distract

EMAIL BEST PRACTICES

We discussed in the last section the basics of structuring your email. Let's now move to email best practices.

Here's what research shows about email best practices:

Best Day

According to an analysis of 500,000 sales emails, emails sent on the weekend are opened 73.6% versus 66.3% during the week and the reply rate is much higher on the weekend as well. We're not saying you should only send emails on the weekend, but it is a strategy you should test.

Best Time

Email follows a similar pattern as phone calls – reply rates are good early in the morning and late evening. 6-7am and near 8pm were the most effective at getting a response, with reply rates hovering around 45%.

Templates

Using templates allows you to actually test your strategies which is key to success.

Links

Don't go overboard with links and attachments, these can get your emails filtered out as spam. One link and one attachment should be enough to get your point across.

Ideal Length

The shorter the better. A Boomerang study showed that emails between 50-125 words had the best response rate at just above 50%.

Sophistication

We all love our buzzwords and industry terms, but the same Boomerang study showed that emails written with a third-grade reading level performed 36% better than those written at a college reading level.

Pictures

Pictures and gifs should be used sparingly.

Number

In our Labs[4] we've found three to be the optimal number of emails. Other studies such as Lead Genius indicate that persistency pays off even up to five emails.

First Call Sequence Structure

Utilize your first call sequence to help you structure your emails, which we'll discuss in later sessions.

Proof is always in the pudding. These are some of the best practices we've witnessed. What are the best practice for your product, industry and audience? Test and you'll find them.

4) INSIDESALES.COM LABS
https://labs.insidesales.com/

EMAIL STRATEGIES

Now that we've covered best practices, let's move to email strategies. Voicemail and email strategies are very similar.

Competition Strategy

Here is an example of an email strategy for competition:

Subject: Some Ideas for Generating More Revenue With Fewer Deals.

Hi John, ABC Company, one of your competitors, was able to generate more sales revenue while working less deals. We'd love to go into the detail with you some time in the next couple of days.

When could we find 5 minutes to connect?

Pain Elimination

Explains how your service solves specific challenges:

Subject: Sales Forecast Driving You Crazy?

Hi John, some of the VPs of sales I have worked with have said, "I just want to know what is going on with the sales pipeline." We'd love to discuss how more visibility into the sales pipeline can improve your sales forecast. When would be a good time to connect?

Research

Use relevant info from external sources to personalize your message:

Subject: Gallup Research for Your Sales Team

Hi John, a Gallup poll reported that employee engagement on the sales floors is at an all-time low at 29%. A lot of sales leaders know they have an engagement problem, but they don't know how to fix it. We have hundreds of clients who are now using TVs with stack rankings and real-time competitions to drive engagement & productivity through the roof.

How's your team's engagement? Do you have time this week to discuss?

These are just examples, of course. It's up to you to personalize to industry and company.

To learn more about email prospecting strategies, watch our webinar[5] with Micheal Pedone, CEO at SalesBuzz.com.

Social Media

With phone, voicemail and email covered the last piece, we'll discuss social. We ran an internal study in the InsideSales.com Labs and it showed that LinkedIn InMail had a 3x response rate in comparison with email. That's powerful! But how do you engage with a prospect via social in a cadence strategy? There are six key skills you need to master.

THE SIX SOCIAL SKILLS (6Cs)

Before you begin using social in a cadence strategy, you need to get the basics of social selling. We believe the 6C's are the basic skills you need to start with.

Complete

The first C is complete. But which platform should you complete? LinkedIn is for B2B business. Facebook is for personal use and consumers, though consumer companies use it well for business. Blogs are the true platform for serious authors and thought-leaders. Twitter amplifies your message. Pinterest and Instagram are visually-focused. Choose wisely.

Purpose: If your purpose on LinkedIn is to promote your business, then don't make it look like an online resume that is trying to get you a job.

Content

If you are a good writer, speaker, or videographer, you can generate your own content. If not, you can do just fine by curating ot her people's content. You can also collaborate with other strong content generators, for improved results.

Value is key. What value do you offer? What stories can you tell? What content can you share to help others? Help people, and respond when others ask questions. If you're not producing a lot of content yourself, you can use content curation sites:

- BuzzSumo
- Bufferapp.com
- Reddit.com
- Hootsuite
- Feedly.com
- Flipboard
- Social networks themselves

Community

You need to connect and target your communities. The best communities are those that already exist with common interest or common experience; here's just a few examples:

- University or alumni groups
- Work groups
- Relevant industry groups
- Trade groups or associations

Comment

Prospects have to know you exist. You have to capture your prospect's attention by making yourself visible to them on social channels. You do this by providing LUV or Leaving Unsolicited Validation.

Each social channel has its way to subtly get on the radar of your prospect. On LinkedIn you can connect, mention, like, share, comment, recommend, endorse, follow, or send an InMail. On Twitter you favorite, reply, retweet, and mention.

If you choose to comment, always be thoughtful. Show that you have read or viewed their content. Don't just make what we call a "drive-by comment."

How do you get others to comment?

- Ask a question.
- Request feedback.
- Stir the pot.
- State a strong opinion.
- Prime the pump with a first comment.

Practice by leaving comments on Facebook posts, blogs, books reviews on Amazon, and articles on Forbes. Invite others to join the conversation. A conversation is the key to engagement.

Connect

Connecting to other people is a skill all on its own. When I first started as a newbie on my own LinkedIn account years ago, I almost got banned for trying to connect to too many people. I soon learned that to connect I needed an existing connection or relationship. They needed to be aware of who I was. You can bridge from other media, messaging, or meetings, voicemail, even email to an immediate follow up in LinkedIn. One of the key ways to get people to connect is to offer content around a mutual common interest or experience.

Call to Action

As the conversation continues, you have to bridge over to a commitment. A Call to Action could mean moving to a more assertive form of communication, such as a phone conversation. You can ask them for small commitments, like joining a webinar or downloading a resource-- or bigger ones like events, or joining a presentation. Too often reps get stuck at this step because it's uncomfortable. Get out of the friend zone and move them to a real prospect by giving them a strong call to action.

APPLYING SOCIAL IN YOUR CADENCE

Okay, so how do you apply the 6cs in your cadence strategy? Focus on the last three Cs. Comment, Connect, and Call to Action.

Interaction 1

COMMENT

Find your prospect on social and show them LUV. Focus on commenting on a post or comment, like something they posted or have done.

Interaction 2

CONNECT

Request to connect. Don't leave the message blank. Ideally, reference some of the LUV from your initial interaction. Or, use an email strategy for an introduction.

Here is an example:

John, I saw you were speaking on the 20/20 panel. I'm excited to tune in as I'm passionate about the topic of 'The Future of Sales."

See you on Wednesday. Gabe

Interaction 3

CALL TO ACTION

Once they have accepted your connection request, you can move to the call to action. Now you can share valuable content and propose a meeting.

Feel free to tailor your interactions to your business. Sometimes you won't be able to find your prospects on LinkedIn, so you may have to skip your social interactions as part of your cadence. Find what works for you and test it.

The thing I love about social is it's different than phone and email. With phone and email, you often are asking for something. On social, you can listen and respond. Listening with intent means you are more likely to be able to start a meaningful conversation with your prospect.

To learn more about social selling, watch our webinar[6], "How to Fit Social Selling into your Sales Cadence."

6) HOW TO FIT SOCIAL SELLING INTO YOUR CADENCE STRATEGY
https://www.insidesales.com/webinar/fit-social-selling-
cadence-strategy/

Direct Mail

These days, it seems like every other sales rep is in love with email. I don't discount its powerful ability to drive business; however, email is just one component of a healthy sales cadence. Our research[7] shows that a full 65% percent of leaders said they are likely to respond to direct mail, and its perceived response rate is higher than that of email.

Direct mail consists of a physical item (note, gifts, etc) mailed to a prospect or customer to initiate a conversation or build a relationship.

Direct mail is useful when you're targeting a select group of people (usually high-ranking executives, managers or directors) in an attempt to create a relationship with the prospect – one that surprises, brings joy or elicits other emotion. It's an outreach tactic for your more sophisticated targets.

Here are some ideas for effective Direct Mail:

- Handwritten cards
- Printed cards
- E-gifts (electronic gifts)
- Small gifts with company branding
- Small gifts without company branding

7) THE STATE OF DIRECT MAIL
https://www.insidesales.com/webinar/state-direct-mail-b2b-leaders-utilizing-direct-mail-win

APPLYING DIRECT MAIL IN YOUR CADENCE

Here are a few tips for creating a rocking direct mail campaign:

Your Gift Doesn't Have to Be Expensive

Some of the most popular and cost-effective direct mailers are handwritten cards, pens, and mugs. This shows you don't have to break the bank to get through to a client.

But Not Too Cheap, Either

The one practice which was most likely to reflect poorly on response rates and the company sending the gift was sending gifts with a perceived value of under $11.

Make it Useful

Useful gifts were much more likely to get a response in our study (47% chance of response) when compared to edible gifts (3.7% chance of a response).

Personalize

One of the most successful sales strategies is personalizing the gift – and the message for your campaign to make sure it fits your target audience. You can do this by segmenting your target audience, using references to industry terms, or simply speak loudly to their pain points.

Example: If you're selling financial services for example, and you're sending a Starbucks coffee gift card, your message could read something like:

"Enjoy a coffee on us, while we work on your accounts."

Want to learn more about direct mail? Watch our webinar[8] with Daniel Gaugler, CMO at PFL.

8) THE STATE OF DIRECT MAIL
https://www.insidesales.com/webinar/state-direct-mail-b2b-leaders-utilizing-direct-mail-win/

Texting

Text messages are no longer just for close friends. Texting can be just as important as any other communication media, when creating a sales cadence. It's a convenient form of communication, that's usually read instantly due to notifications, and allows emojis to make it more personable.

Text messages are very popular outside of the workplace, but they have been gaining ground in the work space as well. Around 62% of people now use texting daily at work, according to a 2017 study, the "Evolution of Business Communication."[9]

Over half of respondents (56%) say they recommend texting as a good way to get ahold of them at work. Texting is more popular among Baby Boomers than Millenials-- but it does carry a sense of urgency, as 3 out of 4 texts are read outside of work.

9) THE EVOLUTION OF BUSINESS COMMUNICATIONS 2017
https://www.insidesales.com/research-paper/
evolution-business-communications-2017/

APPLYING TEXTING IN YOUR CADENCE

So, how do you make texting a part of your sales cadence, without seeming like a creep?

Because texting is so common when talking to family and friends, you need to be careful not to over-use text messages as business communication.

Do's of Texting in Sales:

- Spell-check each and every one of your messages. Nothing's more lame than getting a text from a salesperson about 'premium a offerting."

- Be relevant, concise and to the point. Text messages carry a sense of urgency, so don't over-communicate.

- Send your text at an appropriate time. Every text message has a sound notification, so don't wake up your prospect with a text at 5AM.

Don'ts of Texting in Sales:

- Don't overuse jargon, slang, or get sloppy with your writing. It's supposed to be brief, not bad. One smiley face is OK, but using a lot of emojis is unprofessional.

- Don't cold text your prospects. Texting is more personable and urgent, so use it with people you already have a relationship with.

- Don't spam your prospects. Make sure they are opted in for your messages and provide an exit, or you'll fall foul of the TCPA (Telephone Consumer Protection Act).

You can use text messages when you're already in contact with somebody, and you're coordinating logistics to make sure your deal progresses.

Examples:

- "Just wanted to let you know I'll be meeting you in the lobby"

- "I sent you the updated quote you requested by email, wanted to make sure you saw it"

Example Cadences □-□-⊘

It's important to note that while you may implement certain best practices for your team regarding how and when they follow up with leads, a sales cadence isn't and shouldn't be set in stone.

Once in a while, it's good to analyze your sales cadence for strengths and weaknesses, and find ways to optimize.

Your audience not respoding on the third call? Try a fourth or fifth interaction. Not getting anywhere with voicemails? Try a social media outreach campaign. Certain audiences will respond better to certain media or sequences, and it's up to you to continually test your sales cadence and improve.

Now that we've discussed the five steps on how to build an optimal cadence, let's look at a few examples.

CADENCE EXAMPLE ONE
INBOUND

DAY	CADENCE			SAMPLE DAY
Day 1	✉			Monday
Day 2	📞	☎ voicemail	✉	Tuesday
Day 7	📞	☎ voicemail	✉	Tuesday
Day 14	📞	☎ voicemail	✉	Tuesday
Day 21	📞	☎ voicemail	✉	Tuesday
Day 35	📞	☎ voicemail	✉	Tuesday
Day 49	📞	☎ voicemail	✉	Tuesday
Day 63	📞	☎ voicemail	✉	Tuesday
Day 77	📞	☎ voicemail	✉	Tuesday

📞 = Phone Call   ☎ = Voicemail   ✉ = Email   ⸙ = Social Media

STRENGTHS

- **Lead with Email** - I like the idea of leading with email. That's a strong way to start this cadence based on the audience and the role.

- **Voicemail** - I still believe in VM and I'm glad this team has opted to use it.

WEAKNESSES

- **Same Day** - The obvious problem here is that reps are encouraged to set a task every week. As you can imagine, if you reach out on the same day every time this can be problematic.

- **Spacing** - The spacing of activities is too far apart. We call it the law of immediacy. If you're trying to educate your buyer and you hit them only once a week, they will more easily forget about you.

- **Length** - This is too long. Marketing needs to step in here and enroll this contact in a drip campaign rather than have the rep focus on this contact for 77 days.

- **Social** - In this type of role (relational outbound) social needs to play a part in the cadence.

- **Mix** - I'm a fan of combining phone call, voicemail, and email, but I wouldn't do the same thing every time.

CADENCE EXAMPLE TWO
OUTBOUND

DAY	CADENCE			SAMPLE DAY
Day 1	✉	☎	◯◯	Monday
Day 2	☎			Tuesday
Day 3	☎	◯◯	☎	Wednesday
Day 4	✉			Thursday
Day 7	✉			Tuesday

☎ = Phone Call ◯◯ = Voicemail ✉ = Email ⚗ = Social Media

STRENGTHS

- **Start** - I like the first three days. I think that is a strong start.

- **Mix** - It's good to mix up phone call with voicemail and then phone call without voicemail.

WEAKNESSES

- **Touches** - This is a little weak on the overall touches. I'd at least get 10.

- **Social** - I'm not sure why social was not included in this cadence. For this company it seems to be an obvious thing to do.

- **End** - Ending with two emails is weak. Use more aggressive communication like phone calls.

CADENCE EXAMPLE THREE
OUTBOUND

DAY	CADENCE			SAMPLE DAY
Day 1	✉	✉		Monday
Day 2	✉			Tuesday
Day 3	📞	☎		Thursday
Day 4	⚇	✉		Monday
Day 7	📞	✉	⚇	Wednesday

📞 = Phone Call   ☎ = Voicemail   ✉ = Email   ⚇ = Social Media

STRENGTHS

- **Social** - Good to see social as part of the cadence.

- **Email** - Strong number of emails are being used.

WEAKNESSES

- **Touches** - For a transactional business, this is a little low on the number of touches.

- **Email** - Leading with email is fine, but I wouldn't recommend putting phone calls on day three and starting with three emails.

- **Mix** - This is not enough phone calls. I'd do a minimum of three.

- **Length** - The length is too short. We should push this cadence over two weeks.

- **Voicemail** - I would include another voicemail as part of the last touches.

AI FOR SALES

Score Your Cadence

Wow, this is a lot of information! I realize it might be hard to take this all in-- but I'm sure after a few months practice, you'll be able to master sales cadences in the field.

If you want to know how you're doing, we have a test for that. Our Sales Cadence Audit will compare your team's cadence to those of Fortune 500 companies and tell you how you fare. Do you need to make more phone calls, less social media? Is your duration too short, or are you sending too many emails?

Take our sales cadence audit[11] and find out!

| PHONE | EMAIL | VOICEMAIL | VIDEO | LINKEDIN | DIRECT MAIL |

How Good is Your Cadence?

TAKE THE TEST!

11) https://insidesales.clickfunnels.com/cadenceaudit

AI FOR SALES

Overwhelmed and Tired of Chasing Bad Leads?

Sometimes, sales representatives can get overwhelmed with the sheer number of activities they have to do just to get one single appointment.

Think about it: a minimum of six touches per lead, three communication methods used and answering every lead in the first five minutes is A LOT to keep track of.

Modern sales reps don't manually smile and dial anymore. They use intelligent sales systems powered by artificial intelligence to show them exactly:

- Who the next best prospect is, based on their lead score
- When to call, when to email and what to say to convert them
- Which activities are yielding the best results and how they can get better to increase contact rates.

Try Playbooks, The AI-powered Sales Cadence Tool from InsideSales.com.

12) https://insidesales.com/products/playbooks

Made in the USA
Middletown, DE
14 May 2019